Rocky Runs Away

Written by Sherryl Clark

Illustrated by Andy Elkerton

mountains
cave
forest
animal track
river
village

Contents

Chapter 1

Running Away

Rocky stared up at Dad. He couldn't believe what he was hearing.

"Your wolf cub is getting too big to stay in the village," said Dad. "Tomorrow I'll take him up to the mountains where he can find a wolf pack to live with."

Rocky was so upset that he ran into the hut and put his arms tightly around Alf.

Alf licked his chin.

“I won’t let him take you,” said Rocky. “You’re my friend.” But what could he do?

Rocky thought hard. He and Alf would run away. There was no time to lose.

When Dad went down to the river, Rocky packed some food and his flint knife. Then he went to find his friend, Stubb.

"Alf and I are going away," Rocky said. "Dad doesn't want Alf here any more."

Stubb leapt up. "Can I come?"

"All right," said Rocky. "Bring your snares so we can catch some food." He was glad Stubb was coming – two good friends were even better than one.

Chapter 2

Into the Hills

They set off towards the hills. It was late autumn and the days were getting shorter. They walked and walked, talking and laughing. Alf ran off down side tracks, sniffing and chasing small animals. He ate a small mouse in one gulp!

Soon they were climbing, scrambling over rocks and up steep slopes.

"Ooowwww!" A howl drifted on the breeze.

Alf stopped, his ears pricked up. He whined.

"What was that?" whispered Stubb. He moved closer to Rocky.

"A wolf," said Rocky. "There must be a pack nearby."

Suddenly, Alf darted off, his head high. He disappeared into the woods.

"Alf, Alf!" called Rocky, but Alf didn't come back. They waited and waited. Rocky kept peering into the woods.

"Now what?" asked Stubb. "Maybe we should go home."

"No," said Rocky stubbornly. "Alf will come back. We just have to wait."

Chapter 3
The Cave

It grew dark and things rustled in the shadows. An owl swooped past, its huge wings swishing. Rocky and Stubb ate their food and waited. Stubb jumped at every noise.

As the moon rose, the boys' faces glowed pale in its light. Stubb shivered. "I'm getting tired," he said. "Are we going to sleep here, where a bear might eat us?"

"I don't know," Rocky snapped. He bit his lip and sighed. He wished Alf would come back.

There was a rustle in the bushes – and Alf jumped out!

"Alf!" Rocky grabbed Alf and started to play-wrestle him. Soon, Alf pulled back and trotted away again, but he stopped and looked back.

"He wants us to follow him," said Rocky.

They followed him along the track, and then scrambled up a steep slope. Alf led them to a deep, dark hole in the cliff – a cave.

“I’m not going in there,” said Stubb. “Bears live in caves. There might be one in there, waiting for us!”

Rocky peered into the gloom, then turned to Alf. “Is it safe?” he asked.

Alf ran into the cave and out again, and gave a little yip.

“It’s fine,” said Rocky. He trusted his small friend.

Inside, the cave was cold but dry. They lay down and were so tired that they quickly fell asleep, even though the rocky floor jabbed into them.

Chapter 4

Food!

The next morning, Stubb set his two snares down by the woods. But every time he checked them, they were empty. “There aren’t any hares around here,” he said.

“I’m so hungry,” Rocky complained. “We must catch something, or we’ll have to go home.”

In the distance, a wolf howled again.

Alf stood up, his ears twitching. Then he raced off. Rocky tried to follow him this time but was soon left behind.

When he got back to the cave, Stubb had found a sharp rock and was etching pictures onto the wall.

"This is us," he said, pointing to two figures, "and this is Alf ... and a big bear."

"Stop talking about bears," said Rocky, crossly. He slumped down against the wall. Maybe this time Alf wouldn't come back. Maybe he'd find a wolf pack.

Rocky listened and kept looking at the opening of the cave. Nothing. He grew more and more worried.

Just as Rocky was about to give up, he saw Alf running up the slope. "Look!" he shouted. "Alf's caught a hare!"

They soon had a small fire burning. Rocky skinned the hare and spitted it on a long stick. It sizzled above the flames. The smell of it cooking made their mouths water. Even Alf's tongue was hanging out.

"If we're going to stay here," said Rocky, "we need to catch more game. It's too late in the year for nuts and berries. I'm going to try and make a bow and some arrows. There are some yew trees over there."

"How long are we staying?" asked Stubb.

"Um … a long time," said Rocky. "Until Dad changes his mind."

"That might be forever," said Stubb. "Mum will be worrying about me. Won't your mum worry about you?"

Rocky thought about his mum looking everywhere for him, and maybe even crying. Then he looked at Alf and clenched his fists. No, he wouldn't give up Alf.

"You can go home if you want to," he told Stubb. "I have to stay here with Alf." But in his heart, he wasn't quite so sure any more.

A Terrible Roar

They ate the roasted hare, but it was so small that they still felt hungry.

Rocky jumped up. "I'm going to cut a branch for a bow." He set off down the mountain and Stubb ran after him.

"I'll check my snares again."

The snares were still empty, so they walked towards the yew trees. Just as Rocky reached out to pull down a curved branch and cut it free, a terrible roar echoed through the woods.

A second later, a huge brown bear reared up out of the bushes in front of him.

Rocky froze – his legs wouldn't work.

Stubb backed away. The bear stared right at Rocky and growled, its huge teeth snapping.

Move! Rocky told himself. *Move!* Finally his feet began to retreat but that made the bear growl again and it dropped down on all fours. It took a step towards him.

Rocky's mouth opened but no noise came out. Instead, something else growled, long and low.

"Grrrr!"

Alf brushed against Rocky's leg and thrust his head forward, growling again. His growl said, *Get back, bear.*

The bear stopped. Alf snapped and growled. The bear shook its head.

Then, someone shouted.

"Harrrrrrrr!"

The shout was like a battle cry. A spear whooshed past Rocky and thudded into the ground beside the bear.

This was one surprise too many for the bear. It turned and lumbered away.

Rocky nearly fell over with relief. But who had thrown the spear?

Chapter 6

Rescue

"Rocky!" It was Dad. He pulled Rocky into a big hug. "You were almost bear food then."

"Alf was trying to keep the bear away," explained Rocky in a shaky voice, "but you turned up just in time."

Stubb's dad was there too, smiling with relief. He gave Stubb a big hug.

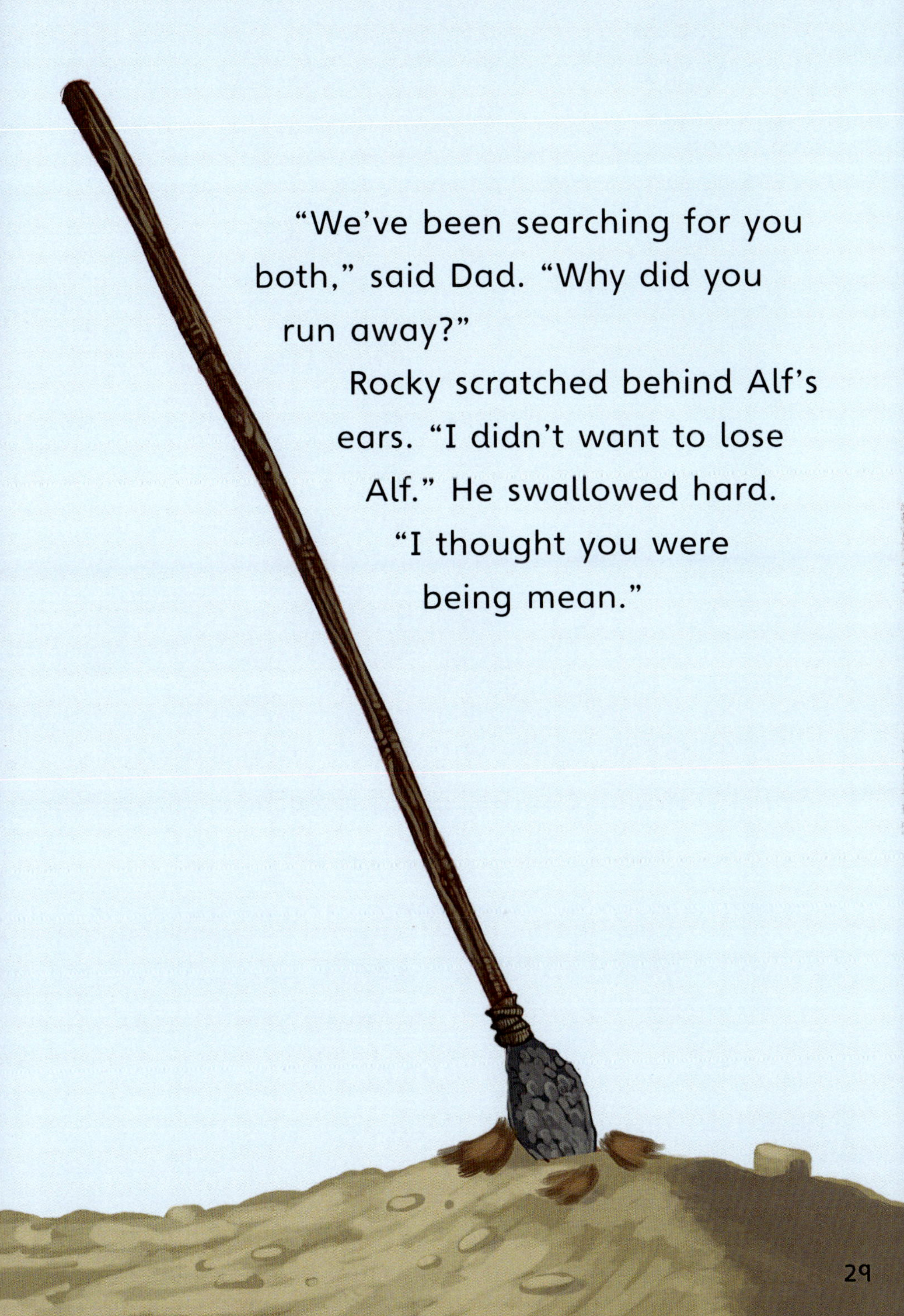

“We’ve been searching for you both,” said Dad. “Why did you run away?”

Rocky scratched behind Alf’s ears. “I didn’t want to lose Alf.” He swallowed hard. “I thought you were being mean.”

“I’m sorry,” said Dad. “But Alf is a wolf, and he doesn’t really belong with us.”

“I know,” Rocky said miserably. “I’ve heard wolves up here, and I think Alf wants to go and join them.”

“Well, he seems happy to stay with you for now,” said Dad. “But one day he will want to leave, and then you’ll just have to let him.”

Rocky nodded sadly.

"Let's go home," said Stubb. "It's been a great adventure but I'm starving. Have we got any eggs or fish at home?"

Stubb's dad laughed and put his arm around his son's shoulder. "I wondered how long you would last without your mum's cooking!"

So they made their way down the mountain and back to the village where the cooking fires were already glowing.

Alf trotted happily at Rocky's heels – for now.